Antipasti and

Small Plates, Trendy and Classic

Contents

Information

Recipes

Appendix

So Easy, So Flavorful

Haven't we all dreamed of going to a restaurant and only ordering appetizers? They all sound so good—sometimes better than the main dishes themselves. Yet, we can't bring ourselves to do it. At home, however, anything is possible. Now you can indulge yourself—and your friends—with small plates from around the world: Italian antipasti, Spanish tapas, and Turkish meze, plus a few Middle-Eastern delicacies.

Small Plate Lingo

1 | Antipasti

Our Italian friends serve up small dishes called "antipasti," literally meaning "before the dough or pasta." In Italian restaurants, they're displayed in an antipasti case and many customers judge the quality of the "ristorante" by the assortment of appetizers available. Antipasti range from some kind of seafood, such as an octopus salad or stuffed mussels to various vegetables, such as bell peppers, mushrooms, and much, much more. In many restaurants, the meal also begins with small bites of crostini—crispy, toasted slices of bread with a wide variety of toppings. For drinks, antipasti are sometimes accompanied by Prosecco (sparkling Italian wine), but more often by a dry white wine.

2 | Tapas

In Spain, early evening means it's time for tapas. This is when many Spaniards make their way directly from work to a bar for an aperitif, accompanied by delicacies known as tapas. These might be as simple as a few slices of ham or chorizo, a little cheese, olives, and salted almonds or more complex like diced chicken in sherry, spicy meatballs, or fried cheese. It's easy to make a meal of these small plates. It's a good thing the Spanish dine later than, for example, the Italians—at about 10 p.m. Drinks served with tapas include chilled sherry and wine (e.g., Spanish rioja).

3 | Mezes

Mezes are Turkish starters that are held in high esteem. They often are part of a "raki table," since Turkish people love their appetizers to be accompanied by raki—a spicy anise-flavored drink that can be consumed on its own or with water. Adding water turns this clear beverage cloudy, resulting in what the Turkish call "aslan sütü" or "lion's milk." In Turkey, family celebrations often involve "only" a meze buffet—all small plates—but they're very extravagant, especially on festive occasions.

➤ **Important:** The amounts in the recipes have been calculated so that a single dish is sufficient for an appetizer. If you want to offer several different appetizers together, alter the amounts accordingly, i.e., make half of a recipe if necessary.

Quick Recipes

Spiced Almonds

SERVES 4:

➤ 2²/₃ cups blanched skinless whole almonds | ¹/₄ cup olive oil | Salt | Hungarian hot paprika

1 | Toast almonds in batches in the hot oil over medium heat until golden.

2 | Return all toasted almonds to the pan, season with salt and paprika, and continue toasting briefly.

Fettunta

SERVES 4:

➤ 8 slices Italian bread | 3 cloves garlic | ¹/₄ cup extra virgin olive oil | Salt (optional)

1 | Toast bread slices in the toaster or oven at 475°F for about 5 minutes until crispy.

2 | Peel garlic cloves, cut in half, and rub onto each bread slice. Drizzle bread with olive oil (or brush on using a pastry brush), and salt lightly, if desired.

Fried Cheese

SERVES 4:

➤ 8 oz whole-milk Manchego cheese | Flour for dredging | ¹/₄ cup olive oil

1 | Remove rind from cheese (discard) and cut rest into long slices about ¹/₄ inch to ¹/₂ inch thick. Dredge in flour.

2 | Pan-fry cheese slices in hot olive oil for about 2 minutes on each side until golden.

Melon Skewers

SERVES 4:

➤ ¹/₂ honeydew melon | 3 oz prosciutto | 3 tbs pitted green olives | 6 cherry tomatoes

1 | Peel melon and cut into cubes.

2 | Cut prosciutto slices in half or in thirds; wrap a slice around each melon cube. Halve the olives and cherry tomatoes. Pierce each piece with a toothpick that has 1 olive or ¹/₂ cherry tomato on it.

5

Preparing Seafood

1 | Mussels

Normally, mussels are already cleaned when you buy them, meaning that the "beard" of dark fibers (that mussels use to anchor themselves to rocks, etc.) has already been removed. But if you see any-thing resembling a beard on the mussels, simply tear it off. Then rinse the mussels thoroughly under cold water and if they're dirty, scrub them with a brush. The mussels' natural reflex is to close their shells. If any remain open, they probably aren't fresh so throw them away. When you cook the mussels, they should all open up. Make sure to discard any that remain closed after cooking. If you're going to bake the mussels in the oven, remove the half of the shell that is empty first and discard it.

2 | Shrimp

Shrimp that you buy raw are normally still in the shell (though it is possible to buy raw shrimp already shelled). Raw shrimp are grayish and cooked shrimp are opaque and pinkish-white. To remove the shell, first pull off the legs, which will loosen the shell and you can slip it off. To remove the tail, pinch it and pull. Make a shallow cut down the back of the shrimp to expose the dark vein, which can be easily pulled out with the tip of a knife. Then rinse the shrimp, dry with paper towels, and proceed with the recipe directions.

> 2 *Slit open shrimp and remove dark vein.*

3 | Sardines & Anchovies

Fatty fish such as sardines are related to herring. If the sardines and anchovies are still very small, people in the Mediterranean region eat them whole, sometimes fresh and sometimes preserved. Both sardines and anchovies (canned) can be rinsed before using them in recipes.

> 1 *Rinse mussels and remove beards.*

Baking Ciabatta

Appetizers are almost never served without bread. So an obvious step would be to try making the bread yourself. If you want, you can also knead pitted black olives into the dough after it rises. It's also nice to add dried herbs such as rosemary or thyme.

Ciabatta

MAKES 1 LOAF:

> - **1 packet yeast**
>   **$1/2$ cup milk**
>   **$5^1/4$ cups flour**
>   **$3/4$ cup whole rye flour**
>   **2 tsp salt**
>   **2 tbs olive oil**
>   **Parchment paper**

TIP

Baking it Crispy
Before sliding the pan into the oven, pour a small cup of water into the oven (or set an ovenproof container of water in the bottom of the oven). The moisture will result in crisping up the bread.

1 Dissolve yeast in milk mixed with about $1^1/4$ cups lukewarm water. Separately, combine both types of flour with salt.

2 Add yeast-milk mixture to flour, then add oil and mix. If dough is too dry, add water (if too sticky, add flour). Knead with a dough hook or your hands to form a smooth dough.

3 Place dough in a bowl and cover the bowl with plastic wrap or a towel. Let rise for 1 hour, until doubled in volume.

4 Preheat oven to 375°F. Shape dough into an oval loaf and place on a baking pan covered with parchment paper. Bake for about 40 minutes.

7

Glossary of Herbs and Spices

Basil: This aromatic herb with an intense scent is available by the bunch. Basil's aroma is stronger if you don't rinse the leaves. If necessary, wipe the leaves with a paper towel and tear them into smaller pieces instead of chopping. If you cut basil too far ahead of time, it will turn black.

Mint: Mint is especially common in Turkish cuisine. There are so many different kinds that it's difficult to specify how much you need for a particular dish. It's best to try a leaf before you decide to use a big handful in one dish—add it into the dish to your taste. If you have some left over, it's better to freeze it than to dry it.

Parsley: This favorite kitchen herb is available in two varieties: Italian (flat-leaf) and the more traditional curly-leaf type. The curly should be used for garnishing and the flat type for flavoring a dish (although both can be used for either). And, cooking doesn't harm this tangy herb one bit.

Thyme: If you have a garden or even a window box, you should grow your own thyme. Thyme plants are much hardier than rosemary and can even survive the winter. Thyme is also an evergreen herb, meaning that it perfumes your kitchen with the scent of fresh herbs even in winter. If you buy it in a bunch and have some left over, tie it into a bundle with string and hang it upside-down to dry; this will retain its wonderful aroma.

Chile Peppers:

Capsaicin is the substance that packs the heat in even the tiniest pepper and is mainly found in: the seeds, the small white ribs of the interior, and some in the flesh of the pepper. If you want to be cautious, buy larger chiles since they're usually milder (but there are exceptions to this rule!). It's best to start out conservatively and add more as desired. Another way to cut down on heat is to omit the seeds and ribs when using chiles.

Garlic:

In the summer, you can buy fresh garlic at the farmer's market; the rest of the year, it's available dried. Always buy plump bulbs and make sure there are no green shoots sprouting out of them. If you find any shoots when you cut them open, always remove them because their flavor is unpleasantly pungent—as is the odor they cause. Garlic cloves with a purple-ish hue to the skin are usually more flavorful than those with the white skin.

Cumin:

This spice is related to caraway but tastes completely different—slightly peppery and even a little bitter. You can buy cumin seed whole or ground. In either case, don't buy too much at a time because spices in particular tend to lose their aroma quickly. You can use an extra grinder to crush the whole seeds for maximum flavor.

Paprika:

Because the tiny peppers used to make paprika are related to bell peppers, paprika is considered a fruit spice. Paprika is available in a very mild form and also in Hungarian sweet and Hungarian hot varieties. The first two are the milder ones and come from a hybrid of hot and mild peppers. Hungarian hot paprika is spicy and can be used in place of chiles.

Finger Food

A glass in one hand, a plate in the other, and the problem is you're supposed to use a fork and knife to eat your food—all while standing up. This dilemma has confounded many a cocktail-party guest. But for situations such as this, there are delicacies threaded onto toothpicks or appetizers so small you can pick them up eat them in one bite. What a fantastic invention!

Quick Recipes

Prosciutto-Wrapped Dates

SERVES 4:

➤ ²/₃ cup pitted whole dates (preferably Medjool) | 1 tbs dry sherry (optional) | 2 tbs freshly squeezed orange juice | 3 to 5 oz thinly sliced prosciutto

1 | If necessary, remove pits from dates. Combine sherry and orange juice and pour over dates. Let stand briefly.

2 | Depending on size of prosciutto slices, cut into halves or thirds. Wrap one piece of prosciutto around each date (reserve the orange juice mixture). In a nonstick pan, sauté wrapped dates over medium heat until crispy. Pour in orange juice mixture and cook to reduce. Remove dates from pan, let cool, and serve with toothpicks.

Cheese Balls

SERVES 4-8:

➤ ³/₄ cup fresh mint sprigs | 2 green onions | 1 fresh red Fresno chile (milder) or red serrano (hotter) | 8 oz crumbled feta cheese | 6 oz cream cheese (or goat cheese or ricotta) | ¹/₂ tsp ground cumin | Salt

1 | Rinse mint, discard stems, and chop rest finely. Rinse green onions and chile pepper and chop both finely.

2 | Finely mash feta with a fork and mix together with the cream cheese, green onions, chile, a fourth of the mint, and all of the cumin (and a little salt to taste).

3 | Shape dough into small balls and roll in remaining mint. Refrigerate for 2 hours.

11

Vegetarian | Fast

Stuffed Tomatoes

SERVES 4–6:

➤ 2 cups large
cherry tomatoes
¾ cup fresh peppery
greens (e.g., arugula
or dandelion leaves)
2 cloves garlic
3½ oz ricotta cheese
3 tbs freshly grated
Parmesan
Salt and pepper
1 pinch cayenne pepper
Basil leaves for garnish

🕐 Prep time: 25 minutes
➤ Calories per serving:
About 85

1 | Rinse tomatoes and cut off tops. Remove contents and finely chop half the contents (discard rest or use for something else).

2 | Sort greens and discard any thick stems. Rinse leaves, shake dry, and chop finely (but save some for garnishing the plate). Peel garlic and squeeze through a press. Combine ricotta, tomato contents, greens, garlic, and Parmesan—then season to taste with salt, pepper, and cayenne.

3 | Fill cherry tomato shells with mixture, garnish with 1 basil leaf each, and arrange on a platter.

Also Delicious Cold

Stuffed Mushrooms

SERVES 4–5:

➤ 16 large mushrooms
1 onion
3½ oz chorizo
(Spanish sausage)
1 tomato
½ cup fresh parsley sprigs
¼ cup olive oil
5 oz ground pork
2 tbs semi-dry sherry
(optional)
Salt and pepper
1 egg
2 tbs breadcrumbs

🕐 Prep time: 40 minutes
🕐 Baking time: 15 minutes
➤ Calories per serving:
About 305

1 | Wipe off mushrooms. Twist off the stems, then dice the stems. Peel and chop onion. Remove the skin from the chorizo (discard) and chop the sausage finely. Rinse tomato and parsley and chop each finely.

2 | In a pan, heat 1 tbs of the olive oil and sauté diced mushroom stems and onions until translucent. Add ground pork and chopped chorizo and sauté until meat is light-colored and crumbly. Add sherry, stir in tomato, and cook uncovered on low for about 5 minutes. Season with salt and pepper. Let cool.

3 | Preheat oven to 425°F. Mix cooled filling with parsley, lightly-beaten egg, and breadcrumbs; use to stuff salted mushroom caps. Lightly grease a baking dish and arrange mush-rooms inside.

4 | Drizzle stuffed mush-rooms with remaining oil and bake in hot oven (center rack) for about 15 minutes. Delicious warm, lukewarm, or cooled.

Photo top: **Stuffed Mushrooms**   *Photo bottom:* **Stuffed Tomatoes** ➤

Inexpensive

Devilled Eggs

SERVES 4:

- 4 hard-boiled eggs
- 1/2 cup fresh parsley sprigs (reserve some for garnish)
- 2 cloves garlic
- 1 tbs capers
- 2 oz canned tuna
- 1 tbs mayonnaise
- 1 tsp tomato paste
- Salt and pepper

🕐 Prep time: 15 minutes
➤ Calories per serving: About 120

1 | Peel eggs and halve lengthwise. Remove yolks and mash with a fork. Rinse parsley and shake dry. Peel garlic. Chop parsley, garlic, and capers until paste-like. Drain tuna and chop very finely.

2 | Combine egg yolks, tuna, parsley-caper paste, mayonnaise, and tomato paste and season to taste with salt and pepper. Use to fill egg halves and arrange on a platter. Garnish with parsley.

Perfect for Company

Stuffed Crispy Olives

SERVES 4–8:

- 5 oz ground pork
- 1 tbs olive oil
- 3 1/2 tbs dry white wine (optional)
- 1/3 cup freshly grated Parmesan cheese
- 2 small eggs
- Salt and pepper
- Freshly grated nutmeg
- 40 very large pitted green olives (imported gourmet type)
- Flour for dredging
- Oil for deep-frying

🕐 Prep time: 40 minutes
➤ Calories per serving: About 265

1 | Sauté ground meat in oil (until cooked through), add wine, and cook until liquid evaporates. Let cool slightly.

2 | To the cooled meat mixture, add Parmesan cheese and 1 of the eggs (lightly beaten) and season with salt, pepper, and a dash of nutmeg. Stuff olives with this mixture (easiest if you use your fingers). Lightly whisk remaining egg. Make sure you have your oil heated before this next step (to 350–375°F, using an oil thermometer). One by one, dredge olives in flour, then dip in egg.

3 | Deep-fry stuffed olives in hot olive oil, drain on a thick layer of paper towels, and serve warm or cold, either cut in half or left whole.

TIP

Stuffing Olives

Even large, pitted olives can have very small openings, which leaves little room for the tasty ground meat filling. In this case, expand the openings very carefully before filling using the thin handle of a mixing spoon. If you have a little filling left over, shape it into small meatballs and fry it along with the olives.

Photo top: **Devilled Eggs**   *Photo bottom:* **Stuffed Crispy Olives** ➤

Vegetarian
Turkish Cuisine

Feta Rolls

SERVES 4–12:
(MAKES 48 ROLLS)

- ¾ cup fresh dill fronds
- ½ cup fresh mint sprigs
- 14 oz crumbled feta
- 2 eggs
- Black pepper
- 1 tsp Hungarian hot paprika
- 6 sheets phyllo pastry
- About 4½ cups oil for frying

🕐 Prep time: 1 hour

➤ Calories per serving: About 365

1 | Rinse herbs and chop finely. Combine crumbled feta with herbs, eggs (lightly beaten), pepper, and paprika. You probably won't need salt because the cheese is salty.

2 | Carefully separate phyllo sheets, stack 2 together at a time, and cut each stack into sixteen rectangles. Distribute a little filling along the wider end of each pastry rectangle. Brush phyllo edges with a little water, roll up into long cylinders, and squeeze ends together well. Repeat with two more batches of phyllo sheet stacks.

3 | Heat oil and deep-fry feta rolls in batches for about 3 minutes until golden brown (at 350-375°F, using an oil thermometer). Remove rolls with a slotted metal utensil and drain well on a thick layer of paper towels. Serve warm or at room temperature.

Transportable

Anchovy Bites

SERVES 4–8:
(MAKES 16 ROLLS)

- 5 green onions
- 2 cloves garlic
- 1 medium-sized potato
- 2 tbs oil
- 8 anchovy fillets (packed in oil)
- 6 eggs
- Salt
- 1 tsp dried thyme

🕐 Prep time: 35 minutes

➤ Calories per serving: About 325

1 | Rinse green onions and slice into fine rings, including the tender green part. Peel garlic and chop finely. Peel potato and grate.

2 | In a large pan, heat 1 tbs of the oil and briefly sauté green onions and garlic. Add potatoes and continue to sauté until potatoes soften a bit. Transfer everything to a bowl. Finely chop anchovy fillets and add. Stir in eggs (lightly beaten) and season with salt and thyme.

3 | Heat remaining oil in pan and pour in the potato-egg mixture. Cook over medium heat until firm. Turn once, then remove from pan, let cool, and cut into 16 narrow pie-shaped wedges. Starting at the wide end, roll up and secure with toothpicks.

Photo top: **Feta Rolls**   *Photo bottom:* **Anchovy Bites** ➤

Prep in Advance | Vegetarian

Falafel

SERVES 4–8:
(MAKES ABOUT
25 FALAFEL)

➤ **1 cup dried garbanzo beans**
1 slice day-old white bread
1 onion
4 cloves garlic
¾ cup fresh parsley sprigs
2 tsp ground coriander
2 tsp ground cumin
Salt and pepper
2 tbs flour
1 tsp baking powder
About 4½ cups oil
for deep-frying
1 lemon

🕐 Soaking time: 12 hours
🕐 Prep time: 45 minutes
➤ Calories per serving:
About 305

1 | Place garbanzo beans in a bowl, cover with a lot of cold water, and let soak for 12 hours or overnight.

2 | Drain garbanzo beans. Crumble bread. Peel onion and garlic and chop both coarsely. Rinse parsley and remove tough stems. In a blender or food processor, coarsely purée the following: bread, onion, garlic, parsley, and garbanzo beans.

3 | Season purée to taste with coriander, cumin, salt, and pepper. In a bowl, mix together with flour and baking powder. Shape mix-ture into walnut-sized balls. (If they're not holding together, add a little water to the purée and mix well.)

4 | Heat oil for deep-frying. To see if it's hot enough, hold the handle of a wooden spoon in the oil. A lot of tiny bubbles should rise around it. Or use an oil thermometer and make sure it reads 350–375°F. Deep-fry the falafel in batches for 4–5 minutes, turning as necessary, until both sides are golden brown. Drain on a thick layer of paper towels. Cut lemon into wedges and serve with the warm falafel.

TIP
Falafel goes well with a spicy sauce. For example: Rinse 1 to 4 green chile peppers (e.g., jalapeño) and chop finely. For less heat, omit seeds and ribs. Peel 2 cloves garlic and chop finely. Combine both ingredients with the seeds of 1 green cardamom pod and crush finely using a mortar and pestle or mini food processor. Season with salt and pepper and stir into ⅔ cup yogurt to make a dip.

Vegetarian

Spinach Turnovers

MAKES 16 TURNOVERS:

➤ **For the dough:**
1³⁄₄ **cups flour**
Salt
1 tbs oil
➤ **For the filling:**
16 oz spinach leaves
3 green onions
1 cup ricotta
1 tsp grated lemon zest
1 egg
Salt
Pepper
Freshly grated nutmeg
➤ **Plus:**
1 egg yolk and 1 tbs milk for brushing on

🕐 Prep time: 50 minutes
🕐 Standing time: 30 minutes
🕐 Baking time: 25 minutes
➤ Calories per turnover: About 90

1 | In a bowl, combine flour with 1 large pinch salt and oil. Mix together with ¹⁄₂ cup lukewarm water; knead briefly to form a smooth dough. Cover and let stand at room temperature for about 30 minutes.

2 | Meanwhile, sort spinach and remove all thick stems. Rinse spinach thoroughly. Do not dry the spinach—place in a large pot, cover, and let wilt over high heat. Pour into a colander and rinse under cold water, drain, and chop finely.

3 | Rinse green onions, trim off root end and any dark green or wilted parts, and cut the rest into fine rings. Combine ricotta, spinach, green onions, lemon zest, and egg and season to taste with salt, pepper, and nutmeg.

4 | Briefly knead dough. Then, on a lightly floured surface, roll out into a thin sheet. Cut into 4-inch squares, put a little filling on each, and fold over into triangles. Press edges together with the tines of a fork (first dipped in flour).

5 | Preheat oven to 350°F. Brush baking sheet with oil. Arrange turnovers on baking sheet side by side. Whisk

together egg yolk and milk and brush on turnovers. Bake in oven (middle rack) for about 25 minutes, until golden. Let cool slightly and serve warm or at room temperature.

➤ **Variations:** Instead of a spinach-ricotta filling, they also taste great with a **meat filling:** Brown 1 lb ground beef in oil with 1 chopped onion and 1 chopped clove of garlic. Combine with 1 tbs pine nuts, 1 tbs raisins, ¹⁄₂ tsp crushed red pepper flakes, and 1 egg. Season with salt and pepper and use as filling.

For a cheese filling:
Combine 7 oz cream cheese (or goat cheese or whole ricotta), 3¹⁄₂ oz grated pecorino, and 1 egg. Chop up a cup of basil leaves and add along with 1 small chopped tomato and 2 tsp rinsed capers and season to taste with salt and cayenne pepper.

Fork Food

Whether it's garlic shrimp, bulgur salad, or mussels, everything in this chapter is designed to be eaten with a fork. The recipes also pair exceptionally well with high-quality artisan bread. Many of the appetizer-like dishes are delicious when served with a dipping sauce. Of course, it's all in the variety—many small plates, all for eating with a fork in hand...but not too much of any one thing. These work great for buffet-style parties where guests can eat while seated.

Quick Recipes

Sausage Meatballs

SERVES 4–6:

➤ **10–12 oz raw Italian sausage** | **$^1/_4$ to $^1/_2$ tsp crushed red pepper flakes** | **1 tbs olive oil** | **$^1/_2$ cup dry red wine**

1 | Squeeze soft sausage out of the skin. Mix with crushed red pepper flakes and form into small meatballs.

2 | In a pan, heat oil and brown meatballs on all sides, until cooked through. Pour in wine and continue cooking until wine has boiled away. Serve warm.

Garlic Shrimp

SERVES 4–12:

➤ **4 cloves garlic** | **$^1/_4$ to $^1/_2$ tsp crushed red pepper flakes (to taste)** | **$^1/_4$ cup olive oil** | **1 lb peeled and de-veined shrimp (raw or cooked)** | **Salt**

1 | Peel garlic and slice thinly.

2 | Heat olive oil and briefly sauté garlic with pepper flakes. Add shrimp. If shrimp are raw, sauté until whitish-pink; if cooked, simply heat. Season with salt and eat with crusty white bread.

Impressive

Vegetarian Artichoke Carpaccio

SERVES 4–6:

- 6 small Italian artichokes
  1 lemon
  1/2 cup fresh parsley sprigs
  1 clove garlic
  1/4 cold-pressed extra virgin olive oil
  6 sun-dried tomatoes, oil-packed type
  Salt and pepper
  2 oz Parmesan (wedge)

🕐 Prep time: 30 minutes
➤ Calories per serving: About 285

1 | Cut stems off artichokes. Remove tough leaves until you come to the tender leaves that you can bite into raw. Halve each and remove thistle-like choke from inside.

2 | Rinse lemon and pat dry. Grate zest off one half, then squeeze out juice from the whole lemon. Rinse parsley, shake dry, and discard the stems. Peel garlic. Finely chop parsley leaves and garlic together.

3 | Whisk together 2–3 tbs of the lemon juice with the olive oil until almost creamy. Slice artichokes lengthwise as thinly as possible and arrange on plates. Sprinkle with lemon zest and parsley mixture. Drizzle with olive oil mixture.

4 | Drain sun-dried tomatoes, cut into strips, and sprinkle over artichokes. Season with salt and pepper. Thinly shave Parmesan over the top using a vegetable peeler.

Traditional with a New Twist | Great for Company

Beef Carpaccio with Arugula

SERVES 4–8:

- 1/2 lb unsliced marbled, high-quality beef
  2 cups arugula leaves (large bunch)
  1 tbs pine nuts
  1/3 cup cold-pressed extra virgin olive oil
  Salt and pepper
  1 lemon

🕐 Prep time: 15 minutes
🕐 Freezing time: 1 hour
➤ Calories per serving: About 230

1 | Wrap beef in plastic wrap and freeze for 1 hour.

2 | Sort arugula and cut off thick stems. Rinse arugula and shake dry. Toast pine nuts in a dry pan over medium heat while stirring until golden; set aside.

3 | Line individual plates with arugula and drizzle with a little oil. Unwrap meat and cut into paper-thin slices with a very sharp knife. Distribute over arugula, drizzle with remaining oil, and season lightly with salt and pepper. Sprinkle with pine nuts. Cut lemon into eighths and serve with carpaccio.

Photo top: **Beef Carpaccio with Arugula**   *Photo bottom:* **Vegetarian Artichoke Carpaccio** ➤

For Company | Easy

Shrimp Frittata

SERVES 4–8:

- **4 potatoes (about 3/4 lb)**
- **5 green onions**
- **1/2 cup fresh parsley leaves**
- **4 cloves garlic**
- **1/2 lb peeled, cooked shrimp**
- **1/4 cup olive oil**
- **Salt and pepper**
- **Hungarian hot paprika**
- **8 eggs**

🕐 Prep time: 45 minutes
➤ Calories per serving: About 535

1 | Peel potatoes, rinse, and slice thinly. Rinse green onions and trim away root end and any dark green or wilted parts; slice rest thinly into rings. Chop parsley. Peel garlic and slice thinly. Thaw shrimp (rinse under cold water) if necessary, pat dry, and chop coarsely.

2 | In a pan, heat half the oil and sauté potato slices over medium heat for about 5 minutes. Add onions and garlic and sauté for about another 2 minutes. Stir in parsley and season to taste with salt, pepper, and paprika to your taste.

3 | In a bowl, whisk eggs and add the following: potato mixture and shrimp. In the large frying pan, heat remaining oil and pour in the egg mixture. Cook frittata over medium heat for about 8 minutes, then use a plate to turn it (and slide it back into the pan); cook another 5 minutes. Serve warm or at room temperature, in wedges.

Also Delicious Cold

Zucchini Frittata

SERVES 4–8:

- **1 lb small zucchini**
- **1 onion**
- **1 clove garlic**
- **1/4 cup fresh thyme sprigs**
- **Several sprigs fresh lemon balm (or Italian flat-leaf parsley)**
- **1/4 cup olive oil**
- **8 eggs**
- **Salt and pepper**
- **2 tbs freshly grated Parmesan**

🕐 Prep time: 40 minutes
➤ Calories per serving: About 460

1 | Rinse zucchini, trim ends, halve lengthwise, and then slice crosswise thinly. Peel onion and chop; peel garlic and mince. Strip thyme and lemon balm leaves from their stems; chop both finely (separately).

2 | In a nonstick pan, heat 2 tbs of the oil and briefly sauté the onion, garlic, and thyme. Stir in zucchini and sauté on medium until crisp-tender.

3 | Meanwhile, whisk eggs slightly. Season with salt and pepper. Stir in lemon balm, Parmesan, and cooked zucchini mixture.

4 | Pour remaining oil into large nonstick frying pan. Pour in frittata mixture and cook over low heat for 15–20 minutes until the underside is set. Use a plate to turn the frittata and slide it back into the pan; cook another 5 minutes. Serve warm or at room temperature, in wedges.

Inexpensive | Spicy

Meatballs in Spicy Tomato Sauce

SERVES 4–8:

- 2 onions
- 4 cloves garlic
- 1/3 cup olive oil
- 1/3 cup semi-dry sherry (or substitute beef broth)
- 1 (28-oz) can diced tomatoes
- 3 sprigs thyme
- Crushed red pepper flakes (to taste)
- Salt
- 1 egg
- 3 tbs breadcrumbs
- 1 lb ground beef

- Prep time: 45 minutes
- Calories per serving: About 570

1 | Peel onions and garlic and chop both finely. Sauté in 2 tbs of the olive oil until translucent. Pour in half the sherry and cook to reduce the amount of liquid. Let cool.

2 | For the sauce: In a pan, combine tomatoes, thyme sprigs, sherry, and crushed red pepper flakes (start with 1/2 tsp flakes and go from there). Cook sauce over low to medium heat for 30 minutes or until thick; salt to taste.

3 | Meanwhile, combine onion mixture, egg, breadcrumbs, ground beef, and salt; mix well. Shape into walnut-sized balls.

4 | In a large pan, heat remaining oil and brown meatballs well on all sides. Pour in sauce mixture (remove thyme sprigs) and stir carefully. Heat thoroughly. Let stand for another 5 minutes and serve.

Easy | Fast

Sherry Chicken

SERVES 4–8:

- 1 lb boneless skinless chicken breast
- 4 cloves garlic
- 1 fresh red Fresno chile
- 1/4 cup olive oil
- 2 tsp Hungarian sweet paprika
- 3/4 cup dry or semi-dry sherry
- Salt
- 1 pinch sugar
- 1 pinch cinnamon

- Prep time: 25 minutes
- Calories per serving: About 350

1 | Cut chicken into bite-size pieces. On a separate board, peel garlic and slice. Rinse chile and cut into fine rings with the seeds.

2 | In a pan, heat oil and stir in paprika. Sauté chicken pieces until golden. Add and briefly sauté garlic and chile.

3 | Pour in sherry. Cook uncovered over medium-high for 8–10 minutes until sherry has boiled down and thickened (also make sure chicken is cooked through). Season to taste with salt, sugar, and cinnamon; serve hot.

Photo top: **Meatballs in Spicy Tomato Sauce**   *Photo bottom:* **Sherry Chicken**

For Company

Roasted Mussels

SERVES 4:

- 2 lbs fresh mussels
  1 cup day-old white bread chunks or crusts
  3 cloves garlic
  ¾ cup fresh basil sprigs
  3 firm tomatoes
  1 egg
  3 tbs freshly grated Parmesan
  Salt and pepper
  2 tbs olive oil

- Prep time: 30 minutes
- Calories per serving: About 135

1 | Rinse mussels under cold running water. Discard any mussels that don't close. In a pot, bring about ½ inch of water to a boil. Add mussels, cover, and cook over high heat for about 3 minutes until the mussels open. Check and if most are still closed, cover, and cook a little longer.

2 | Drain mussels and discard any that are closed. Break off empty shell halves. Place shell halves containing mussels in a baking dish or on a baking sheet. Preheat oven to 425°F.

3 | Crumble bread. Peel garlic, squeeze through a press, and add to bread. Tear basil leaves into tiny pieces. Rinse tomatoes, cut away cores, and dice rest.

4 | Add tomatoes and basil to bread mixture along with egg and Parmesan; mix and season with a little salt and pepper. Distribute this mixture over mussels and drizzle with the oil. Bake mussels on the middle rack for about 5 minutes until slightly brown.

Different

Crispy Whole Sardines

SERVES 4:

- 1 lb small fresh sardines (may substitute whole anchovies; ask your fishmonger)
  2 lemons
  Salt and pepper
  Flour for dredging
  Oil for deep-frying

- Prep time: 25 minutes
- Calories per serving: About 265

1 | Have your fishmonger remove the heads of the small fresh fish, and if they're longer than 4 inches, the bones also. Rinse sardines, including the interior, and pat dry with paper towels.

2 | Rinse lemons and pat dry. Finely grate zest off of one lemon and squeeze out juice. Combine juice with salt and pepper and drizzle over sardines. Mix lemon zest with some flour. Dredge outside of each fish in flour mixture. Knock off excess flour.

3 | In a pot, heat oil. To see if it's hot enough, hold the handle of a wooden spoon in the oil. A lot of tiny bubbles should rise around it. Or use an oil thermometer and make sure it reads 350-375°F. Deep-fry fish for 3−4 minutes while turning with a metal utensil. Drain on paper towels. Cut remaining lemon into eighths and serve with the crispy fish.

Photo top: **Roasted Mussels**   Photo bottom: **Crispy Whole Sardines**

Classic | Italian

Vitello Tonnato

SERVES 6–8:

- 1¹⁄₃ lbs veal round steak (or deboned leg of veal)

  3 cups chopped mixed vegetables such as carrots, celery, leek

  ¹⁄₂ cup fresh parsley sprigs

  1 onion

  1 cup dry white wine (or ³⁄₄ cup water mixed with ¹⁄₄ lemon juice)

  Salt

- For the sauce:

  1 can tuna packed in water (a little over 5 oz drained)

  4 anchovy fillets packed in oil

  1 very fresh egg yolk

  ¹⁄₄ to ¹⁄₃ cup olive oil

  1 tbs fresh lemon juice

  Salt and pepper

  2 tsp small capers, rinsed

⏱ Prep time: 30 minutes

⏱ Cooking time: 45 minutes

- Calories per serving: About 250

1 | Trim away fat from veal. Rinse and chop carrot-celery-leek mixture. Peel onion and halve. Rinse parsley.

2 | In a pot, combine carrots, celery, leek, parlsey, onion, wine, and 4 cups water; bring to a boil. Add veal and immediately reduce heat. Add some salt. Simmer veal over low heat for about 45 minutes until cooked through and then let cool in the stock.

3 | Rinse and drain tuna. For the sauce, purée ¹⁄₂ cup of the cooking liquid with tuna. Drain anchovies, mash with a fork, and stir together with egg yolk. Gradually add oil while whisking constantly until you have a thick mayonnaise. Now add tuna mixture and season sauce to taste with lemon juice, salt, and pepper.

4 | Drain veal and cut into thin, uniform slices. Arrange on plates, pour sauce over the top, and garnish with capers.

TIP

If you don't like tuna, serve the veal with aioli: Make mayonnaise as described using 1 egg yolk and ¹⁄₂ cup olive oil. Peel 4–6 cloves garlic, squeeze through a press, and add. Season to taste with 2 tsp fresh lemon juice, salt, pepper, and Hungarian hot paprika. Delicious with deep-fried seafood as well as with deep-fried or sautéed potatoes and vegetables.

Can Prepare in Advance
Bulgur Salad

SERVES 4:

➤ 1/2 lb bulgur
Salt
5 green onions
3/4 cup fresh parsley sprigs
1/2 cup fresh mint sprigs
4 roma tomatoes
1/2 cucumber
1/4 cup fresh lemon juice
1/3 cup olive oil
Pepper
Cumin (optional)

🕐 Prep time: 30 minutes
🕐 Soaking time: 1 hour
➤ Calories per serving:
About 330

1 | Combine bulgur with 1 cup boiling water and a little salt; soak for about 1 hour.

2 | Rinse green onions and trim away roots and any dark green or wilted parts; cut rest into fine rings. Rinse herbs, shake thoroughly dry, and chop leaves finely. Rinse tomatoes and cucumber and peel cucumber if desired. Dice both very finely.

3 | Combine soaked bulgur with chopped salad ingredients. Stir together lemon juice, oil, salt, pepper, and cumin (if using) and toss with salad.

Vegetarian | Hearty
Zucchini-Olive Pancakes

SERVES 4–6:

➤ 1 lb young zucchini
Salt
1/2 cup fresh parsley sprigs
1 tbs pitted black olives
1 onion
2 eggs
1/3 cup flour
Black pepper
3 tbs olive oil

🕐 Prep time: 30 minutes
➤ Calories per serving:
About 180

1 | Rinse zucchini, trim ends, grate rest finely, combine with salt, and let stand for about 10 minutes.

2 | Meanwhile, rinse parsley and shake thoroughly dry. Remove tough stems and finely chop rest. Chop olives. Peel onion and chop finely.

3 | Water should have formed in the bowl of zucchini. Squeeze out zucchini thoroughly (by first wrapping in cheesecloth or a non-terry dishtowel), then combine with parsley, olives, onion, eggs, and flour and season to taste with salt and pepper.

4 | Heat oil in a pan. Using a tablespoon to measure, form zucchini mixture into small pancakes and fry over medium heat for about 4 minutes on each side until browned. Serve warm or at room temperature.

Photo top: **Bulgur salad**   *Photo bottom:* **Zucchini-Olive Pancakes** ➤

Small Plates with Bread

Anyone who has been to Tuscany remembers the crispy slices of bread with delicious toppings. And then there's bella Italia's tramezzini, toasted sandwiches with a delicate filling cut into convenient triangles. But Spain also makes equally tempting morsels out of bread, and incredible spreads and pastes for topping bread come from Turkey as well. See for yourself!

Quick Recipes

Pan Tomaquat

SERVES 4–8:

➤ 2 large, very ripe tomatoes | 8 (^{1}/$_2$-inch-thick) slices of French or Italian bread | ^{1}/$_4$ cup olive oil | 6 anchovy fillets packed in oil | Salt and pepper

1 | First, you can toast the bread slices (optional). Cut tomatoes in half and rub each bread slice with some of the tomato halves until the tomato is rubbed into the bread; then discard the tomatoes.

2 | Drizzle bread slices with olive oil. Finely chop anchovies and distribute on top. Season with salt and pepper.

Flatbread with Turkish Salad

SERVES 4:

➤ 1 large ripe tomato | 1 red bell pepper | 1 fresh red Fresno chile | 1 small onion | 2 sprigs fresh mint | ^{1}/$_2$ tbs fresh lemon juice | ^{1}/$_4$ cup olive oil | Salt and pepper | ^{1}/$_2$ loaf flatbread (e.g., sesame from Mediterranean market or Italian ciabatta or focaccia)

1 | Rinse vegetables and chile (remove chile stem) and chop all very finely. Finely chop onion. Cut mint into strips.

2 | Stir together all these ingredients with lemon juice and oil and season with salt and pepper. Toast flatbread and top with salad.

Easy | Fast

Prosciutto-Fava Crostini

SERVES 4–12:

- 2/3 cup fava beans (fresh or frozen)

  Salt

  1 tomato

  1 sprig fresh parsley

  2 tbs olive oil

  1/2 tbs sherry vinegar

  Pepper

  12 slices baguette

  12 very thin slices prosciutto (or serrano ham)

🕐 Prep time: 20 minutes

- Calories per serving: About 265

1 | Boil fava beans in salted water for 8 minutes until al dente, rinse under cold water, and squeeze out of white skins (or use frozen, with no need to peel). Rinse tomato and dice. Chop parsley.

2 | Combine fava beans with tomato, parsley, oil, and vinegar and season with salt and pepper.

3 | Toast bread in a toaster or in a 475°F oven (center rack) for about 5 minutes until crispy. Top bread with prosciutto. Distribute fava bean mixture on top.

Fast | Hearty

Tuna Crostini

SERVES 4–6:

- 1 sprig each of parsley, basil, and mint

  2 cloves garlic

  1 can tuna packed in water (5 1/4 oz drained)

  1/4 cup ricotta

  2 tsp fresh lemon juice

  Salt and pepper

  12 slices baguette

🕐 Prep time: 15 minutes

- Calories per serving: About 160

1 | Rinse herbs and shake dry. Peel garlic and chop finely along with herbs until paste-like.

2 | Drain tuna and purée finely with ricotta (in a blender or food processor). Stir in herb mixture and season to taste with lemon juice, salt, and pepper.

3 | Toast bread until crispy, top with tuna spread, and garnish with herbs if desired.

Vegetarian

Bell Pepper Bruschetta

SERVES 4–12:

- 1 yellow or red bell pepper

  2 sprigs fresh thyme

  3 tbs olive oil

  1 tbs capers

  6 sun-dried tomatoes in oil

  Salt and pepper

  12 slices baguette

🕐 Prep time: 25 minutes

- Calories per serving: About 230

1 | Rinse bell pepper, remove stem, seeds, and ribs and dice rest finely. Strip off thyme leaves. Sauté both in 1 tbs of the oil over medium heat for about 5 minutes.

2 | Rinse capers and chop coarsely. Dice tomatoes, combine with remaining oil and bell pepper mixture, and season with salt and pepper.

3 | Toast bread until crispy and top with mixture.

Vegetarian

Marinated Mozzarella Tramezzini

SERVES 4–8:

- 2 green onions
  1 sprig each of thyme, basil, oregano, and parsley
  1 tbs pitted olives
  1/2 tsp crushed red pepper flakes
  2 tbs olive oil
  1 tbs wine vinegar
  Salt
  8 oz fresh mozzarella
  2 large tomatoes
  8 lettuce leaves (iceberg or romaine)
  12 slices sandwich bread

🕐 Prep time: 20 minutes
🕐 Marinating time: 1 hour
➤ Calories per serving: About 305

1 | Rinse green onions and chop finely, including some of the tender green parts. Rinse herbs and chop finely. Chop olives finely. Combine all these ingredients with crushed red pepper flakes, oil, and vinegar; season with salt.

2 | Slice fresh mozzarella thinly. In a shallow bowl, cover with the oil-vinegar mixture and marinate for 1 hour.

3 | Then rinse tomatoes and slice thinly. Rinse lettuce leaves and pare off thick stems so leaves lay flat. Cut crusts from bread.

4 | Top half the bread slices with half the lettuce. Distribute some of the fresh mozzarella on top, then tomato slices, and season with salt. Place bread slices on top and repeat for one more layer. When the top bread slices are in place, cut tramezzini in half to serve.

Can Prepare in Advance

Chicken Tramezzini

SERVES 4–8:

- 12 oz chicken breast
  Salt and pepper
  1 tbs olive oil
  3 1/2 tbs dry Marsala
  1 tbs pitted green olives
  1/4 cup mayonnaise
  1 tsp fresh lemon juice
  1 bunch arugula

  4 marinated artichoke hearts
  12 slices sandwich bread

🕐 Prep time: 35 minutes
➤ Calories per serving: About 380

1 | Season chicken breast fillets with salt and pepper. In a pan with oil, brown well on both sides over high heat. Pour in Marsala and continue cooking over medium heat for 8 minutes, turning as needed. Let cool.

2 | Chop olives. Combine with mayonnaise and lemon juice; season to taste with salt and pepper. Sort arugula, cut off thick stems, rinse leaves, and shake dry. Drain artichoke hearts and slice thinly. Cut crusts from bread.

3 | Slice cooked chicken. Spread bread slices with a little mayonnaise mixture and top with some arugula, artichoke hearts, and chicken; season with salt and pepper. Place other bread slices on top and repeat for one more layer. When the top slice of bread is in place, cut sandwiches in half.

Photo left: **Chicken Tramezzini** *Photo right:* **Marinated Mozzarella Tramezzini** ➤

Can Prepare in Advance

Crostini with Vegetable Spread

SERVES 4–6:

- 1 red bell pepper
  1 yellow bell pepper
  1 fresh red Fresno chile
  1 red onion
  2 tomatoes
  3 cloves garlic
  Salt
  2 tbs olive oil
  1/2 tsp cumin
  12 slices French or Italian bread
- For garnish:
  Canned tuna, olives, capers, and fresh Parmesan or Asiago

- ⏱ Prep time: 20 minutes
- ⏱ Baking time: 30 minutes
- ➤ Calories per serving: About 220

1 | Preheat oven to 475°F. Rinse bell peppers, halve, and remove interiors. Rinse chile and remove stem. Peel onion and cut in half. Rinse tomatoes and cut in half.

2 | Place all vegetables on a greased baking sheet and bake in the hot oven (center rack) for 15 minutes or until the peppers turn dark and develop blisters.

3 | Let vegetables cool. Peel bell peppers and chile. Discard tomato peels as well. Puree all vegetables together (minus the peels).

4 | Peel garlic, squeeze through a press, and add to purée. Stir in olive oil and season with salt and cumin.

5 | To serve, spread thick layer of purée on bread (toasted if desired) and garnish with tuna and/or olives, capers, and hard cheese such as Parmesan.

For the Buffet

Vegetable-Feta Panzanella

SERVES 4–6:

- 3 cups cubed Italian bread
  1 red onion
  1 clove garlic
  1/2 lb tomatoes (about 2 small)
  1/2 lb zucchini (about 2)
  1 bunch parsley
  Several arugula leaves (optional)
  2 tbs wine vinegar
  Salt and pepper
  1/4 cup olive oil
  31/2 oz feta
  1 tbs small capers

- ⏱ Prep time: 20 minutes
- ⏱ Marinating time: 1 hour
- ➤ Calories per serving: About 255

1 | Dice bread coarsely. Peel onion, quarter, and then cut into fine strips. Peel garlic and mince. Rinse tomatoes and zucchini, trim stems and ends, and dice rest. Rinse parsley and arugula (optional) and chop finely.

2 | Combine bread with onion, garlic, herbs, and vegetables. Stir together vinegar, salt, and pepper. Whisk in oil. Toss dressing with bread salad, cover, and marinate at room temperature for 1 hour.

3 | Before serving, crumble feta and rinse capers. Stir salad once more. Serve sprinkled with feta and capers.

Fast | Vegetarian

Hummus

SERVES 4–6:

- 1 (15-oz) can garbanzo beans
  1 clove garlic
  3 tbs fresh lemon juice
  2 tbs olive oil
  3 tbs tahini (sesame paste)
  Salt
  Cumin
  Hungarian hot paprika for sprinkling

⏱ Prep time: 10 minutes

- Calories per serving: About 170

1 | Place garbanzo beans in a colander, rinse under cold water, and drain well. Peel garlic and chop coarsely.

2 | Finely purée garbanzo beans, garlic, lemon juice, oil, and tahini in a blender or food processor. If the cream is too thick, stir in 1–2 tbs water. Season to taste with salt and cumin; sprinkle with paprika.

Vegetarian | Fast

Bell Pepper-Walnut Pesto

SERVES 4–6:

- 1/2 lb red bell pepper
  1 clove garlic
  1/2 cup walnuts
  2 slices sandwich bread
  3 tbs olive oil
  Salt
  1/2 tsp harissa (more to taste)

⏱ Prep time: 15 minutes

- Calories per serving: About 185

1 | Rinse bell peppers, halve, and remove stems and interior. Cut 1/8 of a pepper into fine strips. Chop remaining peppers coarsely. Peel garlic. Set aside 3–4 nice walnut halves.

2 | Process remaining walnuts, chopped bell peppers, garlic, bread, and olive oil in a blender or food processor. Season to taste with salt and harissa and transfer to a serving bowl. Garnish with bell pepper strips and walnut halves.

TIPS

Harissa

Harissa is a fiery hot paste made from red chiles, vinegar, oil, cumin, and coriander. Since the mixture differs a little each time, not all harissa tastes alike. You can buy it in tubes or small cans in Middle-Eastern or Turkish markets. The tube type tends to stay fresher longer. If you buy harissa in a can, transfer it to a screw-top jar and refrigerate.

Tahini

Tahini is a paste made from ground sesame seeds available salted or unsalted. Usually you'll find a layer of oil on top of the paste in the jar. It's best to leave this oil in the jar because it protects the tahini against drying out and keeps mold from forming.

Photo top: **Hummus**   *Photo bottom:* **Bell Pepper-Walnut Pesto** ➤

Fast | Fresh

Avocado Spread

SERVES 4–8:

- 1 large avocado
  1 large, firm tomato
  $1/2$ bunch mint
  1 fresh red Fresno chile
  2 tbs tahini (sesame paste)
  3 tbs fresh lemon juice
  Salt and pepper

- Prep time: 15 minutes
- Calories per serving:
  About 175

1 | Cut avocado in half lengthwise and remove pit. Spoon out flesh and mash finely with a fork.

2 | Rinse tomato and dice finely. Rinse mint and shake thoroughly dry. Finely chop leaves. Rinse chile, discard stem, and cut rest into fine rings.

3 | Combine avocado with tahini and lemon juice. Stir in tomato, mint, and chile pepper. Season to taste with salt and pepper. Serve with bread.

Can Prepare in Advance

Eggplant-Feta Spread

SERVES 4–6:

- 2 eggplant (about 1 lb)
  7 oz feta
  $1/4$ cup olive oil
  2 tbs fresh lemon juice
  2 cloves garlic
  Salt and pepper

- Prep time: 20 minutes
- Baking time: 30 minutes
- Calories per serving:
  About 220

1 | Preheat oven to 475°F. Rinse eggplant, place on a greased baking sheet, and bake in the hot oven (center rack) for about 30 minutes until tender.

2 | Finely crumble feta. Let eggplant cool slightly. Cut in half and remove flesh from peel. Finely purée eggplant flesh with olive oil and lemon juice in a blender or food processor. Squeeze garlic through a press and add. Stir in feta. Season with salt and pepper. Serve with bread.

Inexpensive Vegetarian

Potato-Basil Spread

SERVES 4–6:

- 1 russet potato
  (about $1/2$ lb)
  6 cloves garlic
  $3/4$ cup fresh basil sprigs
  $1/4$ cup olive oil
  2 tbs fresh lemon juice
  Salt
  Cayenne pepper

- Prep time: 35 minutes
- Calories per serving:
  About 195

1 | Boil potato in the peel until tender when pierced with a knife. When cooled, peel and mash. Meanwhile, peel garlic. Discard basil stems and chop leaves coarsely. Purée basil and garlic with the oil in a blender or food processor.

2 | Stir oil mixture into mashed potato and season with lemon juice, salt, and pepper. Serve with bread.

Easy Small Plates

Are you wanting to invite friends over but you hate spending all day in the kitchen? Sometimes, preparing for a party only results in the host being completely stressed out by the time the guests arrive. But it doesn't have to be that way. These recipes are designed for you. They can be prepared in advance, and then when the time comes, all you'll have to do is set the table!

Quick Recipes

Marinated Olives

SERVES 4–8:

➤ 1 lemon | 2 cloves garlic | 1 tsp fennel seeds | 1 tbs parsley leaves | $1/4$ cup olive oil | Salt | 2 cups pitted green olives

1 | Rinse lemon and pat dry. Grate off zest and squeeze juice from one half. Peel garlic and mince along with fennel seeds and parsley leaves.

2 | Combine chopped ingredients with oil and salt. Mix with olives and marinate for at least 2 hours.

Marinated Anchovies

SERVES 4:

➤ 1 bunch parley | A little fresh mint (optional) | $1/2$ tsp crushed red pepper flakes (or to taste) | $3^1/2$ oz anchovy fillets packed in oil | $1/4$ cup olive oil

1 | Rinse herbs and shake thoroughly dry. Finely chop herbs if using.

2 | Drain anchovy fillets, mix with herbs, crushed red pepper flakes, and olive oil; marinate for at least 2 hours. Delicious with grissini (breadsticks), (toasted) bread, or on tomato slices.

Vegetarian
Inexpensive

Marinated White Beans

SERVES 4–8:

➤ 2 tomatoes

1 red onion

2 mild Anaheim peppers
(or mild banana peppers)

1 (15-oz) can white beans,
drained

3 tbs red wine vinegar

1/4 cup olive oil

Salt and pepper

1/4 cup tahini
(sesame paste)

2 tbs fresh lemon juice

1 tbs pitted black olives
(optional)

🕐 Prep time: 20 minutes

🕐 Marinating time: 4 hours

➤ Calories per serving:
About 230

1 | Rinse tomatoes and dice finely. Peel onion and mince. Rinse peppers, halve, remove interiors, and cut rest into fine strips. Drain white beans and mix with chopped vegetables.

2 | Whisk vinegar, oil, salt, and pepper; stir into bean mixture. Marinate for about 4 hours.

3 | Mix tahini with about 1/2 cup water until smooth. Season to taste with lemon juice, salt, and pepper. Distribute salad on plates, sprinkle with olives if desired, and serve tahini dressing on the side.

Easy | Vegetarian

Sherry Onions

SERVES 4–8:

➤ 1 lb shallots (may
substitute small onions)

Several sprigs fresh thyme

2 tbs olive oil

1/4 cup sherry vinegar

1/4 cup semi-dry sherry

1 tbs honey

Salt

Hungarian hot paprika

🕐 Prep time: 20 minutes

🕐 Marinating time: 4 hours

➤ Calories per serving:
About 105

1 | Peel shallots or onions and cut larger ones in half. Rinse thyme, shake dry, and strip off leaves.

2 | In a pot, heat oil and sauté onions and thyme. Add sherry vinegar and sherry, season to taste with honey, salt, and paprika and cover and cook for about 10 minutes.

3 | Let onions cool in the sauce and marinate for at least 4 hours.

Photo left: **Marinated White Beans**   *Photo right:* **Sherry Onions** ➤

For Company
Vegetarian

Garlic Mushrooms

SERVES 4–6:

➤ 1 lb oyster mushrooms (or button, cremini, or mix)
¾ cup fresh parsley sprigs
6 cloves garlic
¼ cup olive oil
Salt and pepper
1 tbs pitted green olives
2 tbs white balsamic vinegar (or white wine vinegar)
1 tomato

🕐 Prep time: 30 minutes
🕐 Marinating time: 4 hours
➤ Calories per serving: About 135

1 | Preheat oven to 475°F. Wipe off mushrooms with paper towels and remove stems. Finely chop parsley. Peel garlic and cut into thin matchstick strips.

2 | Combine mushrooms, parsley, garlic, and oil, season with salt and pepper and place in a baking dish. Bake in the oven (center rack) for about 10 minutes, stirring/turning once.

3 | Remove mushroom mixture from baking dish or sheet. Chop olives coarsely and combine with vinegar and 2–3 tbs water. Pour into baking dish, loosen pan residues using a wooden spoon, and pour this mixture over the mushrooms. Marinate for at least 4 hours.

4 | To serve, finely dice tomato and sprinkle over mushrooms.

Traditional
For the Buffet

Marinated Bell Peppers

SERVES 4–8:

➤ 4 red bell peppers (or 2 red and 2 yellow)
4 cloves garlic
2 tbs white wine vinegar (or fresh lemon juice)
¼ cup olive oil
Salt and pepper
Parsley or basil leaves (optional)

🕐 Prep time: 45 minutes
🕐 Marinating time: 4 hours
➤ Calories per serving: About 120

1 | Preheat oven to 475°F. Rinse bell peppers, halve, and remove interiors. Place on a greased baking sheet with the cut sides down and bake in the oven (center rack) for about 15 minutes or until the peels form black blisters.

2 | Remove from the oven, cover peppers with a damp cloth, and let stand briefly. Peel garlic and cut into fine matchstick strips.

3 | Slip peels off of peppers and cut rest into strips about ¾ inch wide. Combine garlic, vinegar, and oil. Add any juice from the baking sheet that formed from cooking the peppers. Season marinade to taste with salt and pepper and mix with bell peppers. Marinate at room temperature for at least 4 hours. If desired, sprinkle with chopped parsley or basil.

Photo top: **Garlic Mushrooms**   *Photo bottom:* **Marinated Bell Peppers** ➤

Vegetarian

Spicy Eggplant Salad

SERVES 4–8:

➤ 2 medium eggplant (about 1 lb)

2 cloves garlic

1 red onion

1 tsp crushed red pepper flakes (or to taste)

1/4 cup olive oil

Salt

1 bunch parsley

3 tomatoes

Juice from 1 lemon

1 tsp cumin

1 tsp Hungarian hot paprika

1 tsp sugar

🕐 Prep time: 50 minutes

➤ Calories per serving: About 155

1 | Preheat oven to 425°F. Rinse eggplant, trim ends, and dice rest finely. Peel garlic and onion. Chop garlic finely. Halve onion and cut into fine strips.

2 | Combine eggplant, onions, garlic, crushed red pepper flakes, and oil in a baking dish, season with salt, and bake in the oven (center rack) for about 30 minutes, stirring well twice.

3 | Meanwhile, finely chop parsley. Rinse tomatoes, remove cores, and dice rest.

4 | Combine eggplant mixture, parsley, and tomatoes; season with lemon juice, cumin, paprika, and sugar, with more salt to taste. Serve cooled.

Inexpensive

Spicy Carrots

SERVES 4:

➤ 1 red bell pepper

1 fresh hot red chile pepper (serrano, red jalapeño)

1 lb baby carrots

Salt

1 orange

2 cloves garlic

1/2 cup fresh parsley sprigs

2 tbs white wine vinegar

1/2 tsp cumin

1/4 cup olive oil

🕐 Prep time: 30 minutes

🕐 Marinating time: 4 hours

➤ Calories per serving: About 120

1 | Rinse bell pepper and chile (wear gloves when working with chiles), halve, remove stem and interiors, and cut rest into fine strips. Peel carrots and cut into slices about 1/4 inch thick. In a pot, bring a little salted water to a boil, add carrots, cover, and cook for about 5 minutes. Add bell and chile peppers and cook for 3 minutes more or until carrots are crisp-tender.

2 | Meanwhile, rinse orange, pat dry, grate off zest, and squeeze out juice. Peel garlic, rinse parsley, and finely chop both ingredients.

3 | Combine orange juice, garlic, parsley, and vinegar and season with salt and cumin. Whisk in oil. Drain carrots and mix with marinade. Marinate for about 4 hours.

For Company | Low-Cal

Marinated Shrimp

SERVES 4–6:

- 1 lb raw, peeled, and de-veined shrimp
- 1 fresh red Fresno chile
- 1 onion
- 2 tomatoes
- 3 tbs olive oil
- 3 1/2 tbs dry sherry (may substitute fish stock)
- 1/4 cup fresh lemon juice
- A few threads saffron
- Salt and pepper
- 1 pinch sugar
- Fresh cilantro leaves (or parsley)

🕐 Prep time: 25 minutes
🕐 Marinating time: 4 hours
➤ Calories per serving: About 185

1 | Rinse shrimp and pat dry. Rinse chile, remove stem, and cut rest into thin rings. Peel onion, halve, and cut into strips. Rinse tomatoes, remove cores, and dice rest finely.

2 | In a pan, heat oil and sauté shrimp on both sides until cooked through (opaque and pinkish in color), then remove. Pour sherry into pan and, using a wooden spoon, stir, scraping up any residue from the bottom of the pan. Add chile, lemon juice, and saffron; reduce slightly. Season to taste with salt, pepper, and sugar.

3 | Combine shrimp, tomatoes, and onion with marinade and marinate for about 4 hours. Sprinkle cilantro leaves over shrimp.

Impressive

Octopus and Celery

SERVES 4–8:

- 3/4 lb octopus tentacles (or squid)
- Salt
- 3 stalks celery
- 1/2 cup fresh parsley sprigs
- 4 cloves garlic
- 1 lemon
- Black pepper
- 1/4 cup olive oil

🕐 Prep time: 1 hour
🕐 Marinating time: 4 hours
➤ Calories per serving: About 185

1 | Rinse octopus (or squid), place in a pot, and cover with water. Add salt and bring to a boil. Cover pot halfway with the lid and cook over medium heat for about 30 minutes until tender. If it can't be easily pierced with a knife, cook it a little longer. Let cool in the liquid.

2 | Meanwhile, rinse celery, trim ends, and slice crosswise thinly. Rinse, dry, and finely chop parsley. Peel garlic and mince. Rinse lemon and pat dry. Using a zester, grate fine strips off the peel (avoid the white part which is bitter; set zest aside).

3 | Squeeze juice from lemon, mix with salt, pepper, and olive oil and whisk until almost creamy for the marinade. Remove octopus from cooking liquid; cut into bite-size pieces. Mix with marinade, celery, parsley, garlic, and lemon zest; marinate for at least 4 hours.

Photo top: **Marinated Shrimp**   *Photo bottom:* **Octopus and Celery** ➤

Small Plates for Parties— Buffet Style

There's nothing more appealing than a variety of appetizers when you're having a party or large group of guests. Everybody loves "small plates" and almost all the dishes are easy to prepare. You can even ask people to bring something along, such as a dessert.

Choose dishes that can be prepared in advance. See below for examples of winning combinations. As far as possible, do the main shopping several days ahead of time. The day of the party, you need only buy the delicate produce items and the fresh bread. Also, don't forget to buy the little items that make a party special:

grissini (breadsticks), marinated olives, sun-dried tomatoes in oil, and pickles such as cornichons. Per person, plan on $1/4$ to $1/3$ loaf of Italian or French bread, about $1/2$ bottle of wine or 2 bottles of beer, $1/2$ bottle of sparkling water, and $1/4$ bottle of fruit juice or some other soft drink.

WINNING COMBINATIONS

Italian-Style Evening
✗ Tuna crostini, chicken tramezzini, marinated bell peppers, stuffed tomatoes, spinach turnovers, zucchini frittata, beef carpaccio with arugula (or vitello tonnato), octopus and celery

Spanish-Inspired Evening
✗ Prosciutto-wrapped dates, prosciutto-fava crostini or crostini with vegetable spread, stuffed mushrooms, meatballs in a spicy tomato sauce, sausage meatballs, sherry onions, spicy carrots, marinated bell peppers, garlic shrimp, sherry chicken

Festive Turkish Evening
✗ Flatbread with Turkish salad, feta rolls, falafel, zucchini-olive pancakes, bulgur salad, avocado spread, spicy eggplant salad, marinated white beans

Setting the Table

Choose a site where people won't have to jostle one another. Think about where the guests will naturally gravitate. Position the plates at the beginning of the buffet, with the cutlery, napkins, and bread at the end. This allows guests to have their hands free as they make their way through the buffet.

1

Decorating the Table

2

To really show off the various dishes, don't overload the buffet table. A few pretty floral arrangements, individual blossoms (for example, in wine glasses), lemons or even artichokes in a bowl, or colorful fall leaves are more than sufficient.

Chilling Beverages

Place white wine in a large waterproof tub and set it up where no one will trip over it. Fill the tub half full of ice-cold water and ice cubes and place the bottles inside. Chill sparkling water, beer, and soft drinks in the same way. Chill red wine in the refrigerator (yes, we mean it) for 30 minutes prior to the party and then remove (to mimic cellar temperature at serving time).

3

Using this Index

To help you find recipes containing certain ingredients more quickly, this index also lists favorite ingredients (such as shrimp and bell peppers) in bold type, followed by the corresponding recipes.

ABBREVIATIONS	
lb	= pound
oz	= ounce
tsp	= teaspoon
tbs	= tablespoon

The Author

Cornelia Schinharl lives near Munich, Germany. She studied foreign language extensively before devoting herself to nutrition. She received her training as a culinary writer under a well-known food journalist, and worked for a major publishing house in Hamburg. She became a f reelance editor and author in 1985. She is now the author of several cookbooks.

The Photographer

Kai Mewes Kai Mewes is an independent food photographer in Munich, Germany who works for publishers and in advertising. His appealing photography reflects his dedication to combining visual arts with culinary pleasure.

Photo Credits

Cover photo: FoodPhotographie Eising, Martina Görlach
Photos: Teubner Foodfoto (pages 6, 7, 8, 9), Kai Mewes (all others)

Published originally under the title Antipasti und Tapas © 2002 Gräfe und Unzer Verlag GmbH, Munich. English translation for the U.S. market © 2003, Silverback Books, Inc.

Food Editor: Kelsey Lane

Managing editor: Birgit Rademacker

Editor: Tanja Dusy

Reader: Elizabeth Penn, Margit Proebst

Typesetting and production: Patty Holden and EDV-Fotosatz Huber/ Verlagservice G. Pfeifer, Germering, Helmut Giersberg

Printed in Korea

ISBN 1-930603-32-0

Enjoy Other Quick & Easy Books

Marlisa Szwillus

Fondue

Cheese, vegetable, meat kinds of meat, mushroom all kinds at the table, spicier than bbq recipes

Cornelia Adam

Salads

An array of salads to eat at appetizers, entrees, and party buffets. Includes classic choices and cutting-edge alternatives

Sandwiches

Scrumptious, easy snacks and creative fillings.

Xenia Burgtorf

Cornelia Adam

Quiche

Delicious, with simple variations, vegetables, meat, poultry use now-serve for all occasions

Cornelia Adam

Garlic

Sophisticated recipes with the flavor Spice of the cooking Spicy flavor, fine delicate, international

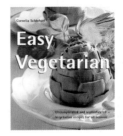

Cornelia Schinharl

Easy Vegetarian

Uncomplicated and sophisticated – Vegetarian recipes for all seasons

Sebastian Dickhout

Casseroles

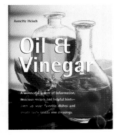

Annette Heisch

Oil & Vinegar

A wonderful source of information, delicious recipes and helpful hints – rich in your favorite dishes and multi tasty foods and dressings.

Andreas Fürtmayr

Sushi

Classic ideas from Japan and new flavor ideas home-made perfection.

SILVERBACK

1 Noodle, 50 Sauces

Everyday Pasta • Old and New Italian Dishes Noodle biography • 10 Tips for Success

SILVERBACK

Healthy Wok

Elisabeth Döpp Christian W Trier Jorn Rebbe

Great flavors and satisfying meals

SILVERBACK

Antje Gruener

Grilling

Crisp, flavorful and fresh vegetable morsels from the grill for your favorite food, from quarrels to down-to-earth classics, with sauces and chutneys

SILVERBACK

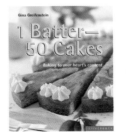

Gina Greifenstein

1 Batter— 50 Cakes

Baking to your heart's content

SILVERBACK

Cooking in Clay

Healthy Recipes with Great Flavor

Erika Casparek-Türkkan

SILVERBACK

Doris Muliar

Cocktails for Drivers

100% Enjoyment

Antipasti and Tapas

Mediterranean Appetizers
Cornelia Schinharl

SILVERBACK

Soups

Classic to Contemporary

Sebastian Dickhout

SILVERBACK

Claudia Schmidt

Raclette

New Recipes with Cheese, Primer and Party Dips

CLEANING CHILE PEPPERS

➤ When you chop hot chiles, the spiciness sticks to your fingers. So avoid rubbing your eyes or they'll burn painfully. Better yet, wear a pair of thin rubber gloves when chopping chiles.

Guaranteed Success for Antipasti and Tapas

NOT TOO COLD

➤ Even dishes that have to be marinated or stored in the refrigerator should always be removed about 1 hour before the meal. They don't develop their full flavor potential until they reach room temperature.

RAW EGGS

➤ The risk of salmonella forming is especially high during hot temperature days. So treat raw eggs with caution. For mayonnaise, the eggs must always be very fresh and the sauce should either be served immediately after preparation or kept in the refrigerator. Do not serve raw eggs to children, the elderly, or those with compromised immune systems.

FAT FOR DEEP-FRYING

➤ You don't have to throw it away after one use. After the oil cools, pour it through a fine strainer to remove all residue and then pour it back into the bottle. If it no longer smells fresh, throw the oil-filled bottle in the trash. Don't pour it down the drain!